This is a collection of poems about nature. It will delight city and country dweller alike for its insight into the subtle connection between things physically observed and things meta-physically felt:

> Let us praise the morning
>   raining birdsong,
> The leaves that move like mobiles
>   in the light,
> The light that falls from the leaves
> Like water flowing over sand,
> The wind and light in the leaves
> Like water flowing over stone,
> And the air that flows like light
> Till light and leaves are one.

Seven of the poems in this collection were first published in *The New Yorker*, to which Mr. Norman has been a contributor since its inception. His poetry has appeared in a number of other leading magazines and literary journals, including *The American Mercury, Harper's Bazaar, Mademoiselle, Saturday Review* and *Nature*.

... remained in Greenwich Village until his recent move to Newport, Rhode Island. He has been an instructor in Shakespeare at New York University. Among his books are four previous volumes of poetry; biographies of Shakespeare, Christopher Marlowe, Samuel Johnson, Ezra Pound and E. E. Cummings; lives of Thoreau and John Muir for young people; and a memoir, POETS AND PEOPLE.

THE PORTENTS OF THE AIR

THE
PORTENTS
OF
THE AIR
AND OTHER POEMS

by Charles Norman

THE BOBBS-MERRILL COMPANY, INC.
Indianapolis/ New York

ISBN 0-672-51407-9 hardcover
ISBN 0-672-51870-8 paperback
Library of Congress catalog card number 77-187009
Designed by A. Christopher Simon
Manufactured in the United States of America

First printing

NOTE

We thank the following publications for permission to re-
print some of the poems that appear in this book: *The New
Yorker* for "A Poem in Praise" (1952), "The Wood: Two
Octaves" (1957), "The Trees, the Birds" (1956), "The Leafy
Air" (1966), "Deserted Farm" (1929), "Death, Look to Your
Domain" (1943), and "The Thin Rain" (1929); *American
Mercury* for "The Portents of the Air" (1948); *Mademoiselle*
for "The Littlest Stars" (1945); *Nature Magazine* for "Ferns
and Fish" (1957); *Panache* for "In the Beginning" (1969);
Queen's Quarterly for "Comprehension of Magic" (1945);
Saturday Review for "The Lake" (1953); *The American-
Scandinavian Review* for "The Deer"; and *Harper's Bazaar* for
"Robin-Walking Time," "Autumn," and "The Dusk Made by
the Snow."

FOR DIANA

CONTENTS

THE PORTENTS OF THE AIR

A POEM IN PRAISE

Let us praise the morning raining birdsong,
The leaves that move like mobiles in the light,
The light that falls from the leaves
Like water flowing over sand,
The wind and light in the leaves
Like water flowing over stone,
And the air that flows like light
Till light and leaves are one.

Let us praise birds in echelon,
The ballet of pigeons on gravel or grass,
And birds alone morning and evening—
The hummingbird in the columbine,
The scissor barn swallow snipping dusk,
Or the pheasant uttering its hoarse, hollow cry,
Trumpeting that trees are spurting red,
That leaves are ripe as fruit,
And the hills as full of hunters
As fleas in a setter's ear.

The naming of simple things
Is both praise and pleasure:
Crocuses burst like firecrackers;
Sea lavender fills the shore with spray;
Clouds break on the high hills like surf;
The little hills are beavers on a bank,
And the plash of a wave on the beach
Is like the plunge of a diver.

In the glooms and greens of the wood,
Sycamores are scrawled in chalk,
Bare boughs are wisps of light,
Bare trees pen scratches on the sky.
Bell notes ripple the still air

Like pebbles cast in ponds.
Rain swarms over the roof like bees,
But on arched highways gleaming in the rain,
Where lights of cars ride by like lights of ships,
Bright wheels whisper the sea's sound.

Finally, let us praise the moon
That turns green meadows into silver lakes,
And the sun that rises crowing like a cock,
Pecking the mist and growing, to become
A pride of lions in a lair of gold,
And goes down like a ship on fire
Far away in a lagoon of air.

THE PORTENTS OF THE AIR

The dwellers on the earth
Look up to scan the sky;
The portents of the air
Fail; the season is awry.

Time, season are awry;
The portents are not clear;
The sun-dog and the sun
Divide the sky in fear.

The moon, slipped like a stone
Into the pond of night,
Displays a luminous ring
In one huge ripple of light.

Submissive to such signs,
The leaves shrink as before;
The air turns dark and moist;
And still it does not pour.

The air is like a bog;
The walker has to wade;
The sign-seekers look down,
And now they are afraid.

All are proud and afraid,
And ponder what's awry;
Oh, let them ponder long—
It is not earth or sky.

SPRING DAY

The blackest band of night
Fades, the stars stream over
The other side of the world;
Trees stand forth like shades;
A brook flows in its shroud;
Birdsong falls like light,
Making the light aloud.

Mist whispers willows thin
As ferns or curving grass;
Trees throng, the woodland grows;
All through the silver din
Of birds the bright brook flows.

The mist utters a hill,
The woods draw near and old,
With winding brooks bird-shrill,
And willows weeping gold.

CHICKADEES

Feeders hang like hives;
These bees are chickadees,
Alighting with fat feet
From bare or budding trees,
Black-capped, black-bibbed, white-cheeked,
Like clowns on a trapeze,
And giving such a glance,
A spring-enchanted man
Holds out his hand to them.

THREE DAYS, THREE SEASONS

A golden eye stared down;
The soiled, tenacious snow
Grinned a spectral grin,
And sank where winters go.

But now upon the ground
There was more fall than spring,
A time before the last
Lay brown and mouldering.

That fall was raked away
To burn with other years,
And the youngest year of all
Stood forth in yellow spears.

An ice-storm might have passed
To make that bush so bright,
There, at a bend in the road,
Where it stands trapped in light.

It was not ice or snow
That set this jewel there,
But a river of gold
Flowing through the air.

A woodchuck rose and stared,
A chipmunk blinked and smiled,
Crows thought they were eagles,
And the sparrows were wild.

COMPREHENSION OF MAGIC

Think how it comes to comprehend
Magic. The spearmen of the grass
Marshal their disarray,
And bow, bow to the winds that pass,
And take their stand and stay.

A host moves silently through mist;
Birds dripping dew are shrill
To take the paths of air;
Trees like brides stand warm and still,
And suddenly we are aware.

THE LAKE

Massed green and silences
Stand guard around the lake;
Maple and the pensive pine
Both shade and shadow make.

Through windows of the wood,
Glooms and gold are seen,
Long boughs where lightfall lies,
Massed silences and green.

Bright-thighed birch and beech
Crowd down upon the shore,
To wade out of the wood,
Loving the lake more.

The water lies so still,
It could be shadow there
Of the still, blue sky
And the still, white air.

Over its placid depth,
A single bird glides past;
Within its shaded deep
Lie fish like shadows cast.

The water is so still,
It lies like silence there,
The silence of the wood
That treads its soft air.

Thin as ferns and fronds
The woodland settles down,
Drowned in that still pool,
Where stars will stream and drown.

CONNECTICUT

A poet sees the metaphor in all things;
Take this old man framed by an autumn day
On a green acre in Connecticut—
He flutters like an aspen on the lawn;
His face and hands are veined and thin as leaves
Through which the light and cool air almost flow;
He merges with the air before my eyes.

He cannot get enough of the air,
Or is it the light?
He cannot get enough of the leaves,
The whisper and waterfall of light
From leaf to leaf;
But now a thin-edged rustle at his feet
Tells that the year has fallen like a leaf.

Grandchildren descend on him like leaves,
And are gone like leaves;
He does not know pure minds have fixed his image,
Framed by this yellow autumn day,
To give him a long life in memory.

His brain shuffles ideas
Like a record player;
He recalls, like you and me perhaps,
Too many, too urgent things—
The inexplicable past,
The pride and sadness of girls,
The young that go to the young
As birds to the fields of air.

Now he is on the porch:
A spider's brood
Bursts in its web like a silent rocket;

A fawn no bigger than a dog
Lopes across the lawn;
A bounding kitten straddles air
With hind legs arched and framing grass.

Two roosters and a cow-belled goat
Perambulate the grounds together—
A subtle potentate, full of suggestion,
Bearded, with cloven feet,
Flanked by oriental feathers.

Behind him in the house a lamp is lit
To draw night and the old man in;
The day hung over him like a pear,
The evening like a plum;
Now a dream drifts on his face.
He peers at a bird or a brook
Going home at dusk.

THE WOOD: TWO OCTAVES

I

I thought the leaf an ear;
Stock-still I stood
To see a leaping deer
Leap into the wood,
Leaping over air,
Thud with flying feet;
But no deer was there.
I heard my own heart beat.

II

When summer's warblers leave,
A leaf that turns in air
To steep in yellow light
Might be a warbler there;
Or, perched upon the wind,
When other colors stir,
Brown leaves, or mottled brown,
Are what the thrushes were.

FERNS AND FISH

Look at the honey locusts—they're like ferns;
That's Brueghel's sky, bisected by a bird;
Here's moss, and ground pine, and a stand of ferns;
I'll tell you what this little one is like—
A princess sleeping in her hair. She turns!
There are the big ones, the big fiddleheads,
Like an enchanted orchestra, asleep;
The wind will soon conduct them with cool hands,
And then the grass, in regiments of green,
Will march and countermarch across the fields.

A wind is springing from the placid pond,
Where a swan drifts, with arctic wing half-spread,
Proud and alone, a mirror for a mate;
A host of silver glitters on gray rafts
Moves silently to take the farthest shore,
Escorted by determined fish below,
So formally maneuvering within,
That the wrinkled pond ripples to a grin.

GRACE NOTE: THE POND

When fish do squads right,
The pond has to grin;
They are so formal,
Maneuvering within,
So proper and precise,
Wigwagging tail and fin,
That the placid pond
Ripples to a grin.

THE TREES, THE BIRDS

Gold air, which cannot hold
A wind that is half light and heaves
Green branches into glass and gold,
Is raging now among the leaves,
While all about go birds in flight,
Of nothing made but golden light.

Now in panic, now in dance,
The leaves leap and are turned to light—
Or glass, upon another glance—
And once again are lost to sight,
While in and out flash birds untold,
Of nothing made but light and gold.

THE LEAFY AIR

In rain-steeped air the rain
Like crooked fingers ran;
At the trees' twined roots flowed
The fisted flood.

Then came the moon,
Treading on twigs of light;
The moon grew weeds and webs
And turned the window into a pool;
The sky was thatched with stars.

The morning's misty rivers
Are flowing through the trees;
Islands and forelands dissolve,
Water-color meadows, hills of air.

Everything flows—sky, leaves, and air:
A pheasant floats by like a potentate,
A red-wing blackbird glides in like a plane,
A heron drifts like a hanged man
Over the pond.

And now, overhead, the leaves
Cluster like grapes
In the blossoming of the air,
The leafy air.

THE RACES AT MOUNT EQUINOX

They gather to see and be seen,
Which accounts for costumes as well as cars.
The cap, rakish and checkered,
With or without a button,
Is definitely back in these circles;
One half expects to see dusters and veils,
Instead of a dazzle of tanned legs.

The racing drivers are of two sorts:
Those who can take a car apart, have done so,
Who know what makes it tick,
Display the grease stains honorably acquired;
And the immaculate ones,
Quite possibly in the Social Register,
Assuredly with credentials at Abercrombie & Fitch.
Some, with intimations of the outer air,
Prefer space-ship glass to goggles,
Which titillates the small fry in the crowd
Starting to wilt from soda pop and sun;
The adults—faces just as young—
Examine all the entrants seriously,
Remark on an excellent paint job,
Know previous records for the climb,
And the names of all the cars.

Talk about Homer's catalogue of the ships!
Here's Mount Equinox on a Sunday
With its Triumph and Jaguar,
Sunbeam Talbot, Hillman Minx,
Thunderbird and Corvette;
Allard, Cisitalia, Bugatti,
Siata, Ferrari, Maserati,
Alfa Romeo, Doretti;
Mercedes 190 and Bandini,

Lancia, Stanguellini;
The PBX with-a-special-body,
And the Pooper (a Cooper with a Porsche engine).
Now there are whispers in the crowd
Of Pegaso—
Costs $29,000—
Only four in the whole country;
Not among those present.

Up at the starting line
A matador of automobiles,
In checked shorts,
Holding a green flag,
Takes his place,
The sun his spotlight,
And puts on an act which, for grace,
Might be in a ballet;
The ballerina is a sports car.
Checked shorts beckons like a prince;
The car creeps forward to his knee,
Where a curt wave stops it cold.
Manual signals come from the control center;
The green flag dips;
"One-two-three-go!"
Says checked shorts whipping the flag down,
And the motor roars, the wheels spin,
The car shoots upward
Buzzing like a monstrous bee,
Shifts to second,
And is lost around a bend under the clouds.

News of its progress comes over the loud-speaker:
Now it is at the first parking lot
(And picnic grounds),

Now at Little Equinox,
Now at the top, clocked and compared,
While the next car is beckoned into place,
The driver dangling a cigarette,
Not nearly so nonchalant as he looks,
But a handsome devil all the same,
Who darts forward at "three,"
Which pains checked shorts,
While the crowd laughs.
The car backs down,
Submits once more,
Waits for the green flag's final whip,
And is off,
Buzzing.

Patient and imperturbable,
With an ear cocked for his time,
The spectators continue to compare,
Saying the same things over,
And wait for the midday break
To buzz up the hill themselves
In low-slung cars of foreign or domestic make,
Flashing the names of the States
And the badges of international clubs
Through a cool corridor of Vermont.

They will picnic under the trees
To the intermittent buzz
Of racing cars trying for the record—
Citizens of the open world,
Tolerant and American,
To whom the Mechanical Muse has sung.

THE DEER

Between the trees of the wood,
Pace the proud, doomed deer,
All pulse, and tense as an arrow,
If anyone should come near.

But at that hour of day,
When it is neither day nor night,
And the deer steal out of the wood
To the meadow drained of light,

I run to that misty meadow
To see the moonlight make
A silver pool for the deer
On the rim of a silver lake;

And think, I must fall on my knees
To see them standing there,
Breasting the misty tide,
Sniffing the misty air.

THE HAWK

I saw the hawk at nightfall,
Flying low,
Over the trail the hunter had taken homeward,
With a bitter look flying low.

Which was heavier, his heart or the bullet?
The red drops fell like rain through the air,
As he followed, bitterly followed the hunter
Home through the ebbing air.

BLUE JAY

The blue jay is a bully and a thief;
Just look at his low brow—I'm not surprised.
I put out crumbs for juncos, but you'd think
I rang a bell or struck a gong for him:
He's sidling down, zigzagging from the sky,
Looking around as solemn as an owl
At every roost along the way, and then
He's here and uttering his hoarse cry,
One claw on booty like a buccaneer,
And looking like a buccaneer's tattoo.
Vexed and aloof the little juncos stand,
And watch him feast through windows made of air.

ROBIN-WALKING TIME

Two robins are walking their chick;
See it waddle, puffed up and proud,
Wading through a forest of grass,
Under a rain of chirpings loud
To beware! beware! till the passer pass.

The robins scatter, plunge and rise,
And pierce the air with silver cries
To distract the passer passing there;
The chick stands still with unblinking eyes
Under a rain of advice from the air.

Return, O robins, and walk your chick
With its puffed-out breast of speckled brown;
Let not my trespass mar this day;
And when bright signals are raining down,
O little robin, obey! obey!

The goldfinches glide in,
Like rich folks in a limousine;
Nobody molests them,
They are so elegant,
Slumming among the flowers;
But a catbird by the lilac bush,
Dark, handsome, villainously slim,
Cocks a calculating eye.

As for the robin at this time of year,
Twanging the yanked, reluctant worm,
Or commuting from the apple tree, where he nests,
To the cherry tree, where he feasts,
Taking a peck at the catbird while in flight,
Just to give him a good fright,
What with clamorous young,
And a living to get,
He's also lean and trim.

See him standing still,
A polychrome, all line,
Like something carved
By a Pennsylvania Dutchman
Tired of making decoy ducks.

PEOPLE, DOGS, BIRDS

People look like other people,
Dogs look like people,
And now look: squatting on a stump,
A phoebe looking like a frump.

But the *petite* wren
Is quite another hen;
Her work is never done,
Yet she is always cheerful,
As well as attractive,
And sings often, without much of an ear.

There, on the lawn, half hidden by the grass,
Is a chipping sparrow.
O you redhead!
You remind me of someone I once knew,
Who was almost as little as you,
Read nothing but Nick Carter,
And had a pocketful of marbles.
They called him Red.

DROSOPHILA

Fruit fly,
Drosophila, dew-loving,
What are you doing here?
There is no fruit,
And I find it vexing
To see you all day, every day,
Flying about my sink.

But just now,
When you thought you were unobserved,
I stood and looked at you on the kitchen wall,
And saw how very small you are.
A year ago
I would have given you such a swat with the towel,
You would not have known what happened.

This comes of reading
Schweitzer.

SWALLOWS

Nothing flies like a swallow—
What are those dips for, dips and curves,
If not the joy of it, the sheerest joy
Of flying nowhere in particular,
Which only swallows do?

They dip, they curve, their wings open and close,
As if to prove it over to themselves,
Over and over, what those wings are like
That snip and slice the blue,
That turn on arcs of air,
Like skaters doing figure eights on ice.

Their young are born to this exuberance—
See how the swallows' fledglings take to flight,
Whistling and showing off,
Flexing their wings and finding that they are
Really, truly, honest-to-goodness theirs!

PEONIES

The explosion of the peonies in the night
Must have been tremendous, a silent roar;
It strewed the table with curled red and white,
And scattered soft debris on the floor.

Snipped ribbons everywhere! I accuse
An elf, made of air perhaps, who had come and gone,
First putting a finger of air like a fuse
On those proud peonies while I slept on.

FORSYTHIA

Beside a flagstone walk,
A fountain dreams all day,
Of arcs and arches made,
Lightfall, leaves and shade;
It once ran trickling gold,
But now pours tumbling green,
With all that leaves can hold
Of light and shade between
Long stems that bend with light.

The shadow of one stalk,
No longer green, but gray,
Floats in a shallow pool
Of sunlight over slate,
Each leaf precise and cool,
Balanced and delicate;
Exactly poised within
The frame that hovers there,
It is a print in flight,
A picture, three-fourths air,
Made for a mandarin.

THE GARDEN

Shadows that dwell in shadows steal
Into the garden at this hour;
Darkness and dew possess the lawn,
But light still lies on every flower.

At outposts of this gallant strand
Tall tulips close themselves in red,
And stand as stiff as grenadiers
To sentinel the flower bed.

The bloodroots wrap themselves in green
And don white turbans for the night;
The flax lets fall blue sky in bits,
To be renewed before the light.

See how the garden goes to sleep,
In mingled fragrance ranging air,
Like ghosts of flowers almost seen,
Or dream of all the flowers there.

FIELDS

As I came through the fields today,
Grasshoppers flew up like spray;
All around me, far and near,
Bees, like disembodied sprites,
Droned in brief, monotonous flights,
And the dainty-stepping deer,
Wide-eyed and innocent of ill,
Poised to run, but statue-still,
Shook suddenly their sheaths of air,
And were no longer there.

OFFSHORE

Aft
    the wind scudded
Ghost sails ghost wake
The gulls touched wings
With undersea gulls
In the glass of the sea.

Over green acres
Raced the stallion waves
Ankles in foam-flowers
Flanks of lightfall made
Manes of spray.

NATURE NOTES

I

The pale snail leaves a slimy track;
He bears his house upon his back;
He has two thin and rigid horns
Fabulous as a unicorn's.

II

The gnats dance in the light
Like a fountain in flight.

III

The robin is a cavalier;
He comes when spring is here or near;
He hops mechanically by
With yellow bill and staring eye,
Head cocked to hear, beneath the grass,
A worm glide in its secret pass.

IV

Thin as a streak the snake flowed
Like a trickle across the road.

V

The patient mole avoids the road;
He bores a tunnel, bears the load
Of the tunnel on his back,
And the tunnel is his track.

VI

The bird that said "Tweet, tweet,"
I think had never heard
"Hello." I said, "Hello!"
To that sweet greeting bird.

And then it made reply:
"Tweet, tweet," it said again.
"Tweet, tweet" may be "Hello"
To birds if not to men.

VII

It is the burning time of year;
From twinkling greens of moss and fern,
Beneath the arches of the grass,
The woods catch fire now and burn.

Green flame leaps up to bud and bole;
As hot as honey runs the sap;
Warmth marries warmth; the sun pours down
Like gold spilled from a miser's lap.

VIII

Like petals on the ground
The windfalls lay,
For the apple is a rose
And each tree was a bouquet.

IX

Summer is over,
Said the brown clover.

X

Nobody cracks a seed or nut
Like that Old English hatcher of hnutus,
The nuthatch, all right going up,
But coming down does it head first
With a lunatic sideways look
And tail pointing to higher things.

XI

Tail propped against the trunk,
As woodpeckers are wont,
Up or down the Downy bobs head up,
Stitching bark with a zigzag hemstitch hop.

IN THE BEGINNING

Think of all the creatures born to die!
I wonder what God had in His immense mind.
Maybe He was bored—
Another reason would be hard to find.

Some things, of course, must have been fun to make,
And gave Him celestial joy—
The sandpiper, say. Who but God could have turned
A toy into a bird that hops like a toy?

But I think He looked down one day and saw the deer,
And said to Himself, "They are standing so very still,
I'll just alarm them a bit"—
And designed the deer fly, without ill will.

Bored in Heaven He was, just simply bored;
There was nothing to it, really, but a whim
When He turned the first blue-faced baboon around
And brushed a pink behind on him.

Also, I wish He had not been so pleased
With His first working model of a man
That He put it on the market before getting the bugs out,
And all that begatting began.

SUMMER'S END

The air is still; the trees
Stand forth in leaves and light;
The trees spurt red; the hill
Is a forest in flight.

The still air moves; the light
Flutters between the leaves;
Though the heart hate or loves,
Summer is with the sheaves.

Summer is in; look now—
Veined autumn trembled there,
Yellow, and leaf-thin,
In the wavering air.

AUTUMN

What dwells in the woods?
  Russet and rustle;
The leaves are astir with fear—
  Hark to their bustle.

What is abroad in the woods?
  Autumn, the half-breed;
See how the stricken leaves
  Tremble and bleed.

NEW HAMPSHIRE IN AUTUMN
FOLIAGE TIME

The lawn slopes to the wood, and there,
By the birch-fringed wood where the grass ends,
She said "the deer like to frisk, the little deer,"
Meaning fawns on the lawn; and so I had a look,
And saw the turf torn up, as it were a moment ago,
And here and there the hoof-mark arrowheads
Where the does and bucks looked on.
Now I am glad I went, after so many invitations,
All those parleyings on the telephone,
Getting there at last to see my friends,
Flying to them over cotton-candy clouds,
Seeing, far off, horizons of cloud,
Islands and ice floes of cloud,
Shorelines and coastlines made of cloud,
Flying above the cotton-candy cloud-capp'd towns,
And all those mountains packed with bouquets
Where dwell the little deer.

DESERTED FARM

The wind goes there to pasture now,
Lonely, ambling like a cow.
Weeds and dandelions breed
Where golden stalks once burst from seed.

When the farmer left the land,
Ruin raised her magic wand;
The land that was the farmer's pride
Suddenly sickened and died.

THE PLANE

Hearing the plane I looked to see
The smudge of sound upon the sky;
But when I looked I did not see
The plane as it went by.

The woods were ankle-deep in leaves,
But overhead the trees were bare;
The branches were like little ferns
That pools in winter wear.

Long I stood and looked at them,
And never were pools' ferns so fair
As the trees' thin tracery
Upon the winter air.

THE LITTLEST STARS

To see perfection sharp,
Abstract and structural,
Hold out your hand to catch
The littlest stars that fall.

In orbits of the palm,
A little heaven they lie,
Stars that feather and fade,
Lost now to earth and sky.

SNOWFALL

The snow comes down;
It is as though
God said: I will cover
The earth with snow.

I will cover the earth
In quiet white;
It won't take more
Than a day or a night;

And the earth will turn
To an older plan,
As it was before
The coming of man;

As it was before
Man trod the ground,
And the earth sang
As it went around.

PINES

The stallions tossed their manes
In a corral of the air;
Terror had ambushed those
Green horses tethered there.

First came the polar bears,
White pelts in a row,
Straddling green branches
With a span, a hug, of snow.

Then came the tigers,
Pouncing with teeth bare,
Gnawing through the tossing manes
Of those green horses there.

And that brought them down,
Brought them low,
Curled and still upon
The cold, still snow.

THE CROW

The crow's shadow
On the snow
Crossed the meadow
With the crow.

It was a race,
A tug for height,
Bisecting space
In fierce flight.

On the bough
Of a bare tree
Shadow and crow
Met suddenly.

THE TWO ENDS OF THE YEAR

In a parenthesis of new moons,
At one end of the year,
Twenty robins set rose-breasts down
And told that spring was here;
Twenty gallant robins made
A garden in the snow,
Bringing roses for the north
Before a bud could blow.

When crook-legged crickets chirped,
At the other end of the year,
A hundred blackbirds drifted down
And told that fall was here;
Then over the arc of the globe
They steered to brighter skies,
Their bills stuck in the south,
The sun in their eyes.

Preludes of silence in cathedral gloom—
The very air was immemorial;
And as I breathed I thought the street became
The youngest church of God who makes the spring;
And lights were born in sudden windows far,
Like glamour in the mind, O alchemy
Of love and evening air and exultation!
Now in the wind's blowing the hedge of spring
Tugs in the wind's meadow, the wind's riders
Go over the thin hedge, the earth is swarming;
The streams of spring flow silver through my thoughts;
The streets stretch out to air, or laved in light,
Flash bright as washing on a line; and now,
How weary are the young, but gay the old!

The summer's images proliferate,
Though at my window I have but a street,
Who have had woods or water at my door;
And steeped in larger air than streets afford,
The country's images, mountain or shore,
Return like robins or snow down like terns
Whose mingling wings made waves upon the wind
Above the waves of sunlight on the sea.
Even these meager trees expound a lane
From pavement drifting like a pond with leaves
When lamplight lies in shallows after rain;
While houses, lit like pumpkins, lapped by stairs,
Ride bright as ocean liners on night's tide,
In rigid convoy with a flight of stars.

Autumn is here, a water-color world;
How tranquilly the leaves relinquish air,
Descending to the ground like butterflies.
It is the little leaves that are most like

Butterflies, dancing their last sad dance,
Not knowing, dancing down, it is the last.
The big ones seem to launch themselves like birds,
And sail like wounded birds bright with their blood
Upon the last adventure leaves can have
To haven far from tumult in the trees.
Why, it's enough to make philosophers
Even out of dodderers in the sun,
Such as myself on this October day
In love with light and leaves, with earth and sky.

Redolent of ocean, cool as a wave,
The night is sluiced into these streets of stone;
The wind is one more billow of the sea
Plashing spindrift of sound upon the roofs.
Do you not feel these combers of the air,
High, thin, and edged with salt, roll over us?
The world drifts in the fathoms of the sky,
A lighted raft upon a sea of lamps;
Look now, the moon sets sail in its bright tide.
We, too, are sailors of the infinite,
Voyagers in the latitudes of space,
Lonelier than all who once upon the deep
Pointed their prows or held the helm hard down
To lands and islands girt by foam and song.

Music comes through the wall—
What are walls for that fall
When music sounds next door?
What are such bulwarks for?

Sometimes the wind can come
And strike a house like a drum
Making the whole house shake
To bring the sleeper awake.

But that is music to bear:
Pillowed on fathoms of air
He hears the night wind's tread
And stars streaming overhead.

THE ELECTRONIC MAN

I walk in the parking-lot streets
Butting unseen faces,
Trailing reels like spittle.

Those who are always there
When walls cascade
Are everywhere.

The refugees
Vanish in mirrors
Above conspiracies of chairs.

I am wound in a cocoon of sound,
Unheard voices flow
Over, through me, and around.

Faces voyaging in air
Stamp me with a smile or stare,
And through me roar the guns of Navarone.

THE ROSE-WINDOW

This rose blossomed for a thousand years,
Rain beat on it in vain;
Snow that whispered there
Withdrew in white despair.

Round, immense and immemorial,
It was a cartwheel of a rose,
Of glass and gladness made—
How could it ever fade?

It took one wink of an instrument's eye
To spill its petals on the ground
In a monstrous blossoming of sound
And flower of this age of rage.

DEATH, LOOK TO YOUR DOMAIN

I am sick of the horror of men,
Who hate their own kind most;
The earth is three-fourths ruin–
One day it will be all ghost.

It will range through the sky like a skull,
Washed by the wind and the rain;
Since men can outdo death,
Death, look to your domain.

WEST SIDE SUNSET

A cloud is bursting like a rose
To make a sunset after all;
The stillness in the west is loud
Where bags and bursting bags of cloud
Scud before the wind and spill.

Antennae flying tattered clouds
Turn roofs to fiery battlements
And tenements to what Troy was
When that ten-years' war was done
At such a setting of the sun.

LITTLE PEOPLE

They do not have to look up
To give the sky a badge;
Curves curl from fingers' ends,
From chalk and crayon's end;
Design for the sake of design
Confers a daisy sun.

The unexpected is usual;
They live close to pavement,
To puddles, dogs and cats,
In a landscape of draped stilts.

Stepping from street to park
They are also close to grass,
And when they wheel, when they whirl,
They are like birds and leaves,
Each leaf a boy or girl.

SKYSCRAPER IN WINTER

On the fiftieth floor
The walls rang;
The wind wound round the walls
And sang.

The thrust of steel and stone
Changed form,
And was a tree
Amid the storm.

It swayed and shook
And joined its shout
To the tall forest
All about.

THE DUSK MADE BY THE SNOW

Although the snow is falling white,
It turns the afternoon to night.

Into the dusk made by the snow,
I button up my coat and go.

Seven winters have not thinned
The cloth that wards me from the wind.

May others, no more cold than I,
See the snow fall from the sky.

Trees, resigned and still,
The birds forsake you now
That made the bells of song
Ring out from every bough.

Dark and still you stand,
Steeped in the thin air,
More beautiful than trees
That water colors wear.

Brides of the dark days,
O lonely, without leaf,
The hurt that mourns in man
Is hushed before your grief.

THE THIN RAIN

The thin rain does a silver dance,
As it weaves the streets,
As it paces over the ground.

The stumbling elephant of wind
Lunges against the stacks of rain;
The thin stalks of the rain break.

The wind makes sudden trees to grow
Over the meadows of bare stone,
These streets in armor against spring.